DNA & GENETIC ENGINEERING

WITHDRAWN

Robert Snedden

Series Editor
Andrew Solway

Heinemann Library
Chicago, Illinois

W9-AJO-514

Designed by Paul Davies and Associates
Illustrations by Wooden Ark
Originated by Ambassador Litho Ltd.
Printed by Wing King Tong in Hong Kong

07 06 05 04 03
10 9 8 7 6 5 4 3 2 1

Library of Congress Cataloging-in-Publication Data
Snedden, Robert.
  DNA & genetic engineering / Robert Snedden.
    v. cm. -- (Cells and life)
Includes index.
Contents: Nature's way -- Reading the manual -- Protein factories --
Gene control -- Introducing e. coli -- Chopping up DNA -- The split gene
problem -- Hitting the target -- Bacterial benefits -- Turning to phages
again -- Going multicellular -- Nature's genetic engineer -- Designer
plants -- Transgenic animals -- Transgenic applications -- Gene therapy
-- Stem cells -- The consequences of cloning -- Genome mapping -- Genome
challenges.
  ISBN 1-58810-674-8 (HC), 1-58810-936-4 (Pbk.)
  1. Genetic engineering--Juvenile literature. 2. DNA--Juvenile
literature. [1. Genetic engineering. 2. DNA.] I. Title: DNA and genetic
engineering. II. Title. III. Series.
  QH442 .S62 2002
  572.8'6--dc21

                            2001008591

Acknowledgments
The author and publishers are grateful to the following for permission to reproduce copyright material:
p. 4 J. Cummins/FPG;pp. 5, 15,18 G. Murti/Science Photo Library; p. 9 Omikron/Science Photo Library; p. 10 J.L.
Amos/Corbis; p. 11 M. Lewis, University of Pennsylvania Medical Center, /Science Photo Library; p. 12 K.
Lounatmaa/Science Photo Library; p. 13 H. Morgan/Science Photo Library; pp. 14, 16 J. Berger, Max Planck
Institute/Science Photo Library; pp. 20, 41, 43 D. Parker/Science Photo Library; p. 21 J. King-Holmes/Science Photo
Library; p. 22 Biology Media/Science Photo Library; p. 23 M. Fermariello/Science Photo Library; p. 24 S.
Stammers/Science Photo Library; p. 25 P. Menzel/Science Photo Library; p. 26 M. Read/Science Photo Library; p. 27 J.
Burgess/Science Photo Library; p. 28 U. Walz/Corbis; p. 29(t) S. Moulds/Science Photo Library; p. 29(b) E. Young
(Agstock)/Science Photo Library; p. 30 M. Whitaker/Science Photo Library; p. 31 .M Baret (Rapho)/Science Photo Library;
p. 32 M. Iwafuji/Science Photo Library; pp. 33, 34 J.C. Revy/Science Photo Library; p. 35 PA Photos; p. 36 Y. Nikas/Science
Photo Library; p. 37 A. Leonard/Science Photo Library; p. 38 Powerstock Photo Library; p. 39 G. Tompkinson/Science
Photo Library; p. 40 S. Fraser/Science Photo Library; p. 42 BSIP, LA/FILIN Herrera/Science Photo Library.

Cover photograph reproduced with permission of Science Photo Library/P. M. Motta and S. Makabe.

Our thanks to Richard Fosbery for his comments in the preparation of this book, and also to
Alexandra Clayton.

Every effort has been made to contact copyright holders of any material reproduced in this book.
Any omissions will be rectified in subsequent printings if notice is given to the publisher.

Some words are shown in bold, **like this.** You can find out what they mean by looking

in the glossary.

Contents

1 Nature's Way

People have very different views about genetic engineering. Genetically modified (GM) crops such as soybeans that are resistant to insecticides are now widely grown for food. But many people think that eating such foods is risky. The first artificially **cloned** animal, Dolly the sheep, was born in 1997, and there is talk today of cloning humans. However, many scientists think that human cloning would be very risky, and some people believe that cloning of humans should never be done. In this book you will learn about genetic engineering and decide for yourself what you think about this controversial area of science.

What is a gene?

In the simplest terms, a **gene** is an inherited instruction for a particular characteristic. Each **organism** inherits its genes from its parents. For instance, genes control the color of your eyes and the type of hair you have, such as straight or curly, light or dark. Each organism has thousands of genes. Some characteristics are influenced by one or two genes. Eye color, for example, is influenced by just a few different genes. Other characteristics, such as height and intelligence, are the result of the combined effects of many different genes.

Each gene is a part of a very long molecule called **DNA (deoxyribonucleic acid)** found in all living cells. In cells with a **nucleus,** the **eukaryote** cells, the DNA is found within the nucleus. When the cell is dividing, the individual DNA molecules coil up to form structures called **chromosomes.**

Mutations

Each time a cell divides, it makes a copy of its DNA. On rare occasions, a mistake is made and part of the DNA molecule is copied incorrectly. These mistakes in the DNA molecule are called **mutations.** Altered, or mutated, genes can be passed on from a parent to its children.

A child inherits genes from its father and mother. When a child has the same color eyes or hair as a parent, it's the result of these genetic connections.

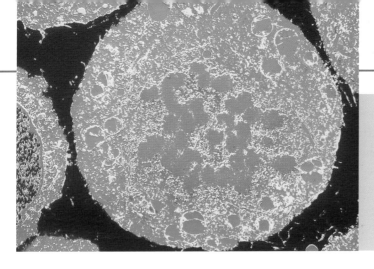

The chromosomes (orange) are clearly visible in the center of the dividing cell. In nondividing cells, the chromosomes are not visible. Magnification approx. x 4,000.

Most of these these changes are small and don't matter much. It would be as if you misspelled one word in a set of instructions, and no one really noticed. Other times, however, the change might alter the whole meaning of a genetic instruction. This could result in the gene doing something entirely different. The result may be disastrous and lead to the death of the organism. Then again, the change might be harmless. It might cause straight hair instead of curly hair. On rare occasions, the change offers an advantage. An animal might be able to run faster, for example, and so escape from its predators.

Random shuffling

We all have a different set of genes that plays a part in making us who we are. You have characteristics in common with your parents, your brothers, and other close relatives because you have many genes in common. But in each person, the mix of genes is different. Only identical twins have exactly the same set of genes.

On the whole, everyone has two versions of each gene, one from each parent. Males and females each produce sex cells. These cells contain only one version of each gene. When these sex cells form, there is some shuffling of the genes. The genes in the parent's chromosomes mix together into new combinations.

A male and a female sex cell combine in a process called fertilization. The fertilized cell is the first cell of a new living thing and has two sets of genes, one from each parent. Fertilization is a random event. There is no plan as to which male and female sex cells will successfully combine to form a new living thing.

The possible number of combinations that can arise from gene shuffling and random fertilization is mind-boggling. There are 10^{600} possible gene combinations that can occur in humans. That is a 1 with 600 zeroes after it. Part of what genetic engineering is about is taking the randomness out of the gene shuffling and taking control of which genes appear in a particular organism. In order to understand how this is possible, we will take a closer look at how genes work.

2 Reading the Manual

A cell's **DNA** can be thought of as an instruction manual for making parts of a cell. Each **gene** is the plan for a particular part. Genes carry instructions for making **proteins.** If the instructions in a gene are followed, a protein will be made.

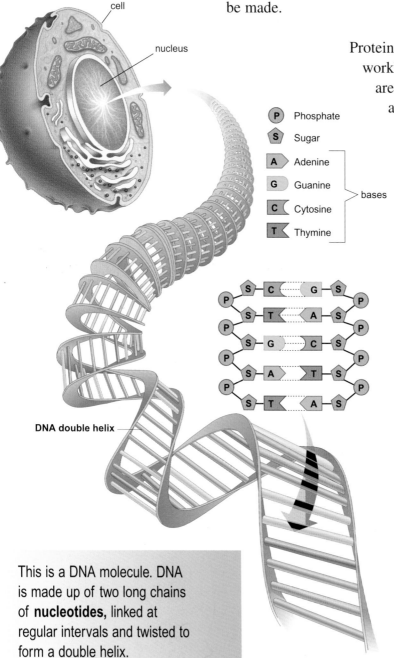

cell

nucleus

P Phosphate

S Sugar

A Adenine

G Guanine

C Cytosine   } bases

T Thymine

DNA double helix

Proteins are the building blocks and workhorses of the cell. Some proteins are parts of the cell structure. Others are **enzymes,** or **catalysts,** that control chemical reactions in the cell. Each reaction in the cell has its own specific enzyme, and because the enzymes control the reactions, they effectively control the cell and the way it develops.

These events at the level of the cell give rise to the characteristics we see in an **organism,** such as pink flowers on a pea plant or curly hair on a child. This process of following a gene's instructions is called **gene expression.**

A cell does not act on all its DNA instructions at once. Different genes are switched on and off as they are needed. This is because DNA isn't just a small instruction manual—it is a cellular encyclopedia. You never read an encyclopedia from cover to cover, you only read those articles that you need at a particular time. In a multicellular organism, such as a plant or an animal, all the cells (except the sex cells mentioned earlier) contain the same DNA. However, there are many different types of cells, and different genes are switched on in each cell type. Every cell in an organism has the same instruction manual, but different cells read different parts of it.

This is a DNA molecule. DNA is made up of two long chains of **nucleotides,** linked at regular intervals and twisted to form a double helix.

DNA and proteins

The goal of carrying out a gene's instructions is to make a protein. Protein molecules are long chains of small subunits called **amino acids.** There are twenty or so different kinds of amino acids. A single chain of amino acids is called a **polypeptide.** A protein may have just one polypeptide, or it may have several linked together.

The order of the amino acids in a polypeptide chain is important. Changing one amino acid for another can affect the way the protein works. This is why it is so important for a cell to follow the instructions for each protein in its DNA.

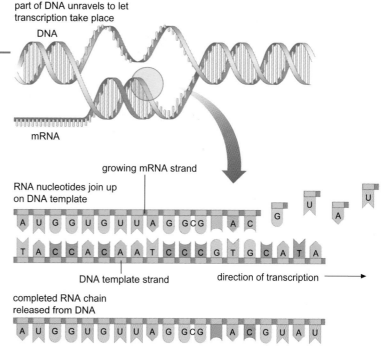

This diagram shows the transcription of a section of DNA to make messenger RNA. The enzyme RNA polymerase joins the RNA nucleotides together. Transcription happens quickly. About 30 new nucleotides are added to the chain each second.

A gene's instructions are written in the structure of its DNA. DNA is made up of two long chains of smaller molecules called nucleotides. It looks something like a spiraling, twisted ladder, with the two chains wound around each other. Chemicals called **bases** link the strands together at regular intervals. It is the order of the bases that indicates the genetic instructions.

There are four bases: adenine (A), cytosine (C), guanine (G), and thymine (T). The bases pair up across the DNA molecule like rungs on a ladder. T is always paired with A, and G with C. The two DNA chains are said to be complementary because the sequence of bases on one strand determines the sequence on the other.

Copying a gene

When a cell wants to make a particular protein, it first has to copy the instructions from the DNA. Copying a gene is called **transcription.** When a gene is transcribed, the DNA molecule unwinds where that gene is located. One strand of the DNA, called the coding strand, acts as a template, or blueprint, for making another molecule, called **RNA (ribonucleic acid)**. RNA is very similar to DNA, but it is made up of a single strand of bases instead of a double strand. Also, one of the bases in DNA, thymine (T), is replaced by another base, uracil (U). This RNA transcript is called **messenger RNA.** It carries the protein-building instructions from the **nucleus** to the **cytoplasm,** where the actual assembly of proteins takes place.

Protein Factories

The next stage in making a **protein** is called **translation.** The order of the **bases** along the **RNA** strand is translated into a series of **amino acids** to be assembled into a **polypeptide** chain.

How can just four bases carry instructions for twenty different amino acids? The answer is that the bases have to be read in groups of three. Each group of three bases, called a triplet or **codon,** stands for a particular amino acid. There are 64 possible codons that can be made with the four bases. Each amino acid is coded for by one or more of these codons. The amino acid lysine, for instance, can be coded as either AAA or AAG. The complete amino acid dictionary is what we call the **genetic code.** The genetic code is the same in all living **organisms,** a fact that is of great importance in genetic engineering.

Reading the code

The actual process of building proteins takes place in structures called **ribosomes.** Here, **messenger RNA** is translated codon by codon to produce a polypeptide chain. A ribosome attaches to a messenger RNA strand at one end. The ribosome then travels along the strand, translating it codon by codon.

Another type of RNA, called **transfer RNA,** plays a vital part in the assembly of proteins. There are different forms of transfer RNA, each of which carries a particular amino acid. A particular transfer RNA molecule binds only to the messenger RNA codon that corresponds to the amino acid it carries. For example, a transfer RNA carrying lysine might only bind to the codon AAA.

This illustration shows how proteins (developing polypeptide chains) are assembled on a ribosome. The messenger RNA is translated by transfer RNA.

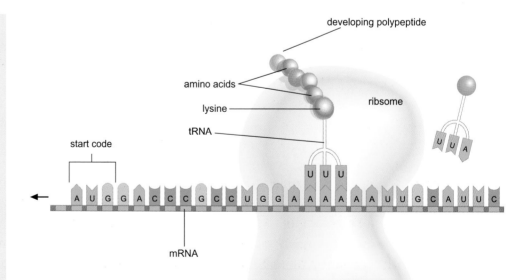

developing polypeptide

amino acids

lysine

tRNA

ribosome

start code

mRNA

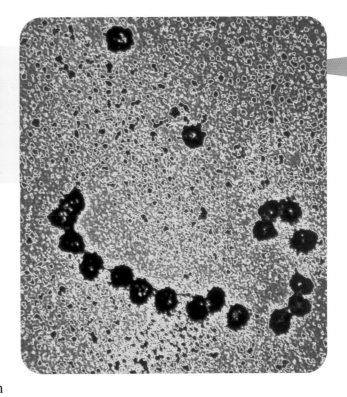

This photo, taken through an electron microscope, shows a number of ribosomes on a single strand of messenger RNA. Magnification approx. x 270,000.

As the ribosome travels along the messenger RNA, a transfer RNA molecule brings the amino acid for a particular codon on the messenger RNA. As each codon is translated, another amino acid is added to the end of the growing polypeptide chain. More than one ribosome can move along a messenger RNA molecule at any one time. In this way, there can be polypeptides at different stages of assembly along the messenger RNA strand, similar to a factory production line.

At the end of the messenger RNA strand is a special codon called a stop codon. The stop codon says, "instructions end—stop assembly." The polypeptide chain is complete and released from the ribosome. It then folds up, perhaps linking with other polypeptides, to form a protein that can go on to fulfill its task in the cell.

Engineering goals

Genetic engineers often aim to transfer **genes** from one organism to another, or to alter genes within an organism. The point of doing this is to introduce new proteins into the organism in order to change what happens in the cell. Changing the genes is more effective than simply injecting an organism with new proteins. Proteins don't last long. They are broken down and recycled. But once a gene has been written into the **DNA,** its instructions can be read again and again to make new proteins. Since DNA is copied from one generation to the next, from parents to offspring, changes in DNA can be carried from one generation to the next.

The fact that all organisms use the same genetic code means that we can transfer genes from one species to another, and the new species will be able to read the genes. The universal nature of the genetic code means that any gene can be decoded by any organism to produce the same protein product. However, as we will see, bacteria can have problems reading **eukaryote** cell genes. But genetic engineers can put human genes in pigs and jellyfish genes in mice.

Gene Control

An **organism's** cells use only some of their **genes.** Different cell types with their different tasks require different **proteins** that have to be constructed according to the instructions on different segments of the cell's **DNA.** Some estimates suggest that the cells of a multicellular organism use only five to ten percent of their genes at any given time. This means that there must be some type of control system in place that prevents genes from being expressed regardless of the cell's needs. A gene that is not expressed has no effect on the cell.

Some genes are expressed all the time because their proteins are involved in vital activities. The **enzymes** involved in **respiration,** for example, are always needed. Other genes may never be expressed, or may be expressed just once in a while. One reason why bacteria are such phenomenally successful organisms is that they can rapidly step up or cut back on the production of enzymes, depending on the nutrients available to them.

Regulatory proteins

The control of **gene expression** is very complex. Genes can be switched on or off by special proteins called **regulatory proteins.** Often, several different regulatory proteins can act on one gene. They may act on the gene site itself to allow **transcription,** or they may block it. They may act at a later stage in the process, controlling production of a **polypeptide** by the **ribosomes.** Or, they may affect the actual polypeptides produced and either activate or deactivate them.

One example of gene regulation was discovered in bacteria more than 30 years ago. A series of genes in bacteria, called lac genes, produces enzymes that can

The genes that code for the production of blossoms in these cherry trees are not expressed until environmental factors, such as length of day, act as a trigger. This means that all the cherry trees in an area blossom at the same time, making it easier for trees to pollinate each other.

break down **lactose,** which provides the bacteria with energy. When there is no lactose available, a regulatory protein called a repressor binds to the bacterial DNA and halts the transcription of the genes. This repressor protein doesn't work if there is lactose in the cell. Therefore, when lactose is present in the bacterial cell, transcription of the lac genes can continue. The lac genes then produce enzymes that the bacterium can use to get energy from the lactose.

Promoters

Like other reactions in the cell, the production of **messenger RNA** from a particular stretch of DNA is controlled by an enzyme. Before this enzyme can work, it must attach to the DNA at a point just before the gene. This site is called a **promoter.** When the enzyme is bound to the promoter site, the gene can be transcribed to produce messenger RNA. Without the enzyme, transcription is not possible.

Unlike the **genetic code** itself, promoters are not universal. Some promoters work in more than one species, but in some cases the enzyme of one species does not recognize and bind to the promoter in another. If this happens, there will be no transcription and no protein building. The gene will not be expressed.

If a genetic engineer wants to transfer a gene from one organism to another, the section of DNA he or she transfers must include the promoter as well as the gene itself. Furthermore, the promoter must be recognized by the binding enzymes in the host organism's cells. If these conditions are not met, nothing will happen.

Some bacteria used in genetic research have enzymes that will readily bind to promoters from a range of other organisms. Other bacteria are quite fussy about the promoters they respond to.

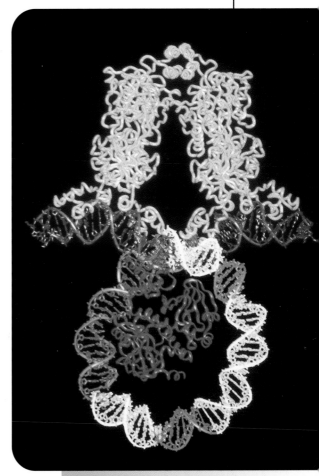

A computer graphic shows the lac repressor protein attached to DNA. The site at which it attaches stops the enzyme RNA polymerase, a promoter, from attaching to the DNA. Magnification approx. x 40,000.

3 The Benefits of Bacteria

The first successes in genetic engineering involved inserting foreign genes into bacteria. This might not seem very useful, because bacteria are extremely small and very simple **organisms.** However, genetically engineered bacteria have been useful in several different ways.

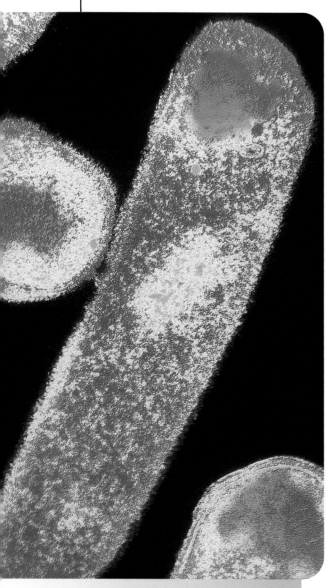

These *Bacillus subtilis* bacteria have been genetically modified to produce a **vaccine.** The red and purple areas in the bacteria indicate the presence of the vaccine. Magnification approx. x 50,000.

Humans have a long history of using bacteria for a variety of tasks. Bacteria are involved in the production of yogurt and cheese, for example. We also get **antibiotics,** the drugs we use to fight off infections, from bacteria. Bacteria have been engaged in chemical warfare with one another for many millions of years. Antibiotics are part of this battle. An antibiotic is a substance that kills or prevents the growth of bacteria. Soil bacteria, in particular, produce antibiotics as part of their natural defenses to kill off other bacterial colonies that grow in the same area.

Hundreds of different antibiotics obtained from a variety of **microorganisms** are in use today. The search for new ones continues, as medical science tries to keep pace with the ability of bacteria to evolve rapidly and gain resistance to everything we can throw at them.

Building better bugs

Genetic engineers are working to make bacteria do things we need even better. One method used in the past was a hit-and-miss approach. This involved causing **mutations** artificially in a colony of bacteria, hoping that some desirable mutation would occur. A more certain way is to isolate **genes** that produce the **proteins** we are interested in and then insert them directly into the bacteria we wish to alter. The ability of populations of bacteria to grow rapidly makes them extremely effective chemical factories for the production of useful proteins.

Drugs from bugs

One protein made in genetically engineered bacteria is used to treat **diabetes.** Diabetes is a potentially serious illness caused by an inability to produce a hormone called insulin. Insulin is a protein involved in controlling the amount of sugar in the blood. Without it, levels of sugar in the blood may vary wildly, causing all kinds of problems. In the days before genetic engineering, people with diabetes were treated with insulin obtained from pigs and cattle. This was not an ideal treatment, because insulin from these animals is slightly different from human insulin. Today, stainless steel vats hold vast populations of *Escherichia coli* bacteria (*E. coli* for short) that have been genetically altered to contain the genes for human insulin. These bacteria represent the first large-scale use of genetically engineered organisms. Today, other medically important proteins are also manufactured by bacteria, including blood-clotting agents, growth hormones, and interferon, a protein that is effective against infections caused by **viruses.**

As yet, scientists have not been able to genetically engineer bacteria to produce antibiotics. Antibiotics are not proteins, so it is not possible to simply insert an antibiotic gene into a bacterium. Instead, genetic engineers would have to insert most or all of the genes that code for the **enzymes** involved in making the antibiotic.

Cleanup squad

Genetically altered bacteria may also be used to deal with pollution. Many bacteria play a vital role as decomposers. They break down dead organisms and recycle organic wastes, making nutrients available for reuse by other living things. Researchers have also been able to genetically engineer bacteria that can break down oil spills and neutralize harmful chemicals that cause pollution. However, these bacteria have only been tested in the laboratory. If they prove to be safe, such bacteria could be effective in cleaning up environmental hazards.

These fermentation vessels are used to grow huge numbers of microorganisms that have been genetically altered to produce substances such as insulin.

4 Inserting New Genes

We have learned about some of the useful jobs that genetically engineered bacteria do for us. But how exactly are these bacteria made? How do genetic engineers put new **genes** into bacteria?

Introducing *E. coli*

E. coli is a common bacterium that lives in the intestines of mammals, including humans. It is mostly harmless and is very easy to keep in the laboratory. Provided with the right conditions, it can divide in two every 40 minutes or so. Scientists have been studying *E. coli* for years, and many genetic engineering techniques have been developed using this **organism.**

Eukaryote and prokaryote chromosomes

Like all other bacteria, *E. coli* is a **prokaryote.** This means that it has no **nucleus.** The cells of all other living things are **eukaryotes.**

The genetic material in bacteria is in some ways different from that in eukaryotes. In eukaryote cells, **DNA** is bound with **proteins** called **histones.** A single molecule of DNA is wound around a number of histones in a complex fashion, making it compact and able to fit inside the nucleus. The DNA is at its most compact during cell division, when the DNA and histone structure becomes visible under the microscope as a **chromosome.**

A magnified photo of rod-shaped *E. coli* bacteria. Magnification approx. x 5,000.

In a prokaryote cell, the DNA is naked, that is, it is not enclosed within a nucleus or bound with proteins to form a chromosome. The prokaryote chromosome is simply a DNA molecule folded inside the cell. The ends of prokaryote DNA molecules are joined, forming a closed loop of DNA. Eukaryote chromosomes do not form loops in this way.

There are about four million **base** pairs in the DNA molecule of *E. coli*. This is tiny compared to the 100 million base pairs in a single human chromosome. Humans have 23 pairs of chromosomes in each cell. When *E. coli* reproduces, its single chromosome loop is replicated, and each new bacterium gets a copy.

Plasmids

In addition to its single DNA molecule, *E. coli* may also have a few smaller loops of DNA called **plasmids,** which can also be passed on at cell division. Plasmids have only a few thousand base pairs. There are various types of plasmids, but generally a bacterium has only one type at any one time. However, it can have many copies of the same plasmid. It is not unusual for a bacterium to have hundreds of identical plasmids. Sometimes a bacterium can have no plasmids at all, which suggests that plasmids are not essential for the bacterium's survival.

The genes on plasmids often give the bacterium resistance to **antibiotics,** which is used to wage war on other bacterial strains. A bacterium that has plasmids is resistant to any attack by antibiotic-producing bacteria.

Plasmids are important in genetic engineering because they can be extracted from bacterial cells. Then they can be readily introduced into bacterial cells that have no plasmids of their own. Plasmid genes can therefore be introduced into bacteria that previously did not have any.

The discovery of the techniques for transferring plasmids from cell to cell was an important step in the development of genetic engineering, but it was only the beginning. A major factor in the advance of genetic engineering came with the discovery of another weapon that bacteria use to defend themselves against attack. This weapon is a special class of **enzymes** that bacteria use to chop up the DNA of an attacking **virus.** These enzymes are called **restriction enzymes.**

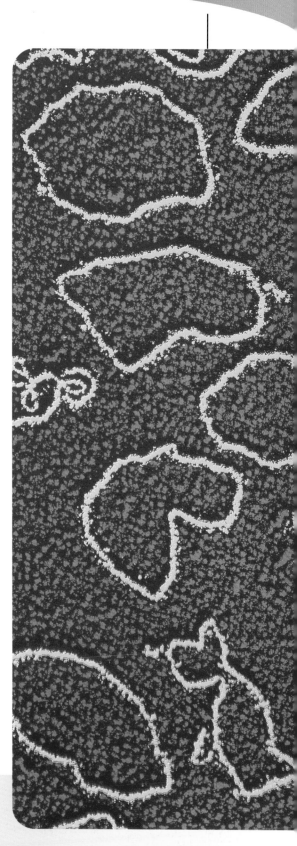

The loops in this photo are plasmids inside an *E. coli* bacterium. Magnification approx. x 80,000.

Chopping Up DNA

Multicellular animals are vulnerable to attack by **microorganisms.** For this reason, they have had to evolve a form of defense against infection. The human **immune system** includes millions of white blood cells which identify foreign invaders and then use various methods to fight them off.

Bacteria, although microscopically small, can get infections from even smaller disease-causing agents called **viruses.** Viruses that infect bacteria are called **bacteriophages,** or simply **phages.** Phages inject their **DNA** into bacterial cells.

Bacteria have a defense system to help fight against viral attack, but their defense system is nothing like our complex immune system. After all, a tiny single-celled **organism** cannot call on millions of white blood cells to attack an invader. Instead, **enzymes** in the bacterium recognize the presence of foreign viral DNA, and other enzymes go to work to chop it into pieces.

This is a scanning electron micrograph of T4 bacteriophages on an *E. coli* bacterium. The restriction enzymes that bacteria use to cut open viral DNA are used by genetic engineers to cut DNA into fragments. Magnification approx. x 31,000.

The enzymes responsible for chopping up a virus's DNA are called **restriction enzymes.** Each type of restriction enzyme recognizes a short sequence of DNA **bases,** called its target sequence. If a foreign DNA molecule has these target sequences, the restriction enzyme cuts through the DNA molecule and splits it into fragments. Each fragment is roughly a gene-sized piece of DNA, around 1,000 to 5,000 base pairs in length, which is just large enough for one or a few genes.

Restriction enzymes and genetic engineering

It is possible to remove restriction enzymes from bacteria and purify them in the laboratory. Many hundreds of enzymes from many strains of bacteria have been isolated, and these make up a genetic engineer's toolbox. They can be used for cutting up DNA and therefore for cutting out genes. Restriction enzymes are what make possible a genetic engineering technique called **recombinant DNA** technology. Using this technique, the genetic engineer can combine DNA from different species.

Recombinant DNA technology is the basis of genetic engineering. Restriction enzymes are used to cut up the DNA from one organism. Then the genes of interest are isolated from the fragments. Restriction enzymes are then used to open **plasmids,** and the genes isolated from the first organism are inserted into these plasmids. The plasmids are then closed up to produce plasmids with foreign **genes** inserted into them. This technique is called **gene splicing.** Plasmids containing foreign DNA are called recombinant plasmids.

E. coli containing plasmids

cells of organism containing genes of interest

molecules of DNA

plasmids

open plasmids

pieces of DNA containing genes of interest

insert and splice in pieces of foreign DNA

recombinant plasmids

treatment with chemicals

plasmid-free *E. coli*

Using restriction enzymes, DNA can be cut into gene-sized fragments. Other enzymes are used to insert the DNA fragments into bacterial plasmids. Bacterial cells are then treated with chemicals to help them take up the engineered plasmids.

A group of bacteria is then treated with the recombinant plasmids. Some of the bacteria take up the plasmids. The bacteria are spread on the surface of a growth medium, a jellylike substance called **agar gel** that contains nutrients that the bacteria can use as food. Then the bacteria begin to divide. As the bacteria divide, soon there is a population of genetically identical individuals, or **clones,** all of which contain a copy of the recombinant plasmid.

The plasmids act as carriers for transferring the genes into the bacteria. These genes can come from any source. They might come from another bacterium, either of the same or another species, or they might come from an entirely different organism such as a plant or an animal.

Split Genes

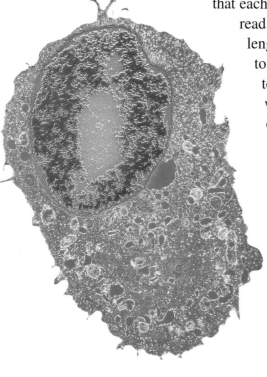

When **DNA** and **genes** were first being investigated, it was assumed that each gene was a continuous section of DNA that could be read and transcribed to give a continuous corresponding length of **messenger RNA.** This would then be translated to give the correct series of **amino acids** to be linked together in a **polypeptide** chain. However, scientists were surprised to find that the truth was a little more complicated.

There is a major difference between the structure of **eukaryote** genes and **prokaryote** genes. Many genes in eukaryote cells are not a continuous sequence of DNA, but are split over several segments. The DNA is not physically split. The long chain of the molecule remains intact. However, the **protein**-making code that comprises the gene is interrupted by sequences of **bases** that do not code for proteins. These noncoding regions within the gene are called **introns,** because they interrupt the code. The coding regions of the DNA are called **exons.** Not all eukaryote genes are split, but some are split spectacularly. The gene for collagen, a protein found in animal tissues such as tendons, is interrupted by nearly 40 introns.

This is the cross section of an animal cell that has been cultured (grown) in the laboratory. Cells like this one are used to produce messenger RNA, from which complementary DNA (cDNA) can be made.

The intron sections of the gene obviously have to be removed before the messenger RNA can be used to manufacture a protein chain. This happens after the messenger RNA has been made from the DNA, but before it leaves the **nucleus. Enzymes** cut out the **RNA** sequences that correspond to the introns and connect the exon sections together again. Once the messenger RNA has been modified, it passes out of the nucleus for **translation** into a polypeptide.

Bacterial genes have no introns. Each gene is a continuous stretch of DNA code with no interruptions. This raises a problem for the genetic engineer. If a eukaryote gene is transferred to a bacterium, and if that gene happens to be a split gene, there is no way for the bacterium to produce a protein from that gene. The bacterium has no machinery for modifying RNA and removing introns from it. If genetic engineers want to introduce a eukaryote gene into a bacterium, they first have to find a way to make the split gene usable.

Intron bypass operation

The solution to this problem is to transfer genes that have already had their introns removed. The eukaryote cells from which the genes are removed are made to do most of the work. Rather than cut up a cell's DNA to get the target gene, the genetic engineer looks for the messenger RNA strand that corresponds to the gene in the **cytoplasm.** This RNA strand will have already had the introns removed. Once the messenger RNA has been isolated, it is used as a template to produce a complementary strand of DNA (cDNA). This cDNA strand is equivalent to the gene minus its introns.

Copying the RNA to give cDNA is the reverse of what happens during **transcription.** Instead of using DNA to make messenger RNA, messenger RNA is used to make DNA. Scientists can cause this reverse transcription to occur in the laboratory thanks to the discovery of an enzyme found in some **viruses.** This enzyme is called, appropriately enough, **reverse transcriptase.**

Reverse transcriptase has a very useful property. When it comes into contact with a messenger RNA strand and a source of **nucleotides,** it assembles a DNA strand that complements the sequence of bases on the RNA. This single DNA strand can then be used as a template to make a second DNA strand with the use of the services of yet another enzyme, known as **DNA polymerase.** The end result is an artificial gene that contains a continuous sequence of coding bases without the introns.

This diagram shows how complementary DNA (cDNA) is made.

Finally, the artificial gene is spliced into a **plasmid** that can be inserted into a bacterium. Once there, the gene can begin to produce proteins.

Hitting the Target

We have seen how it is possible to move **DNA** from one **organism** to another. But how does the genetic engineer ensure that the right DNA segment is being introduced? How can specific genes be isolated and transferred?

Gene libraries

The complete set of **genes** in an organism is called its **genome.** There are nearly 400 genes in the *E. coli* genome, and more than 30,000 genes in the human genome. When genetic engineers want to isolate a gene, they split up the entire genome of a cell containing that gene and incorporate the gene fragments into bacteria by way of **plasmids.** Each of the individual genes from the cell ends up in a separate bacterium. This mixed collection of genetically altered bacteria makes up a gene library of the original organism.

Dishes of **agar gel** support colonies of bacteria that contain recombinant genes.

If we know that a gene we are interested in is somewhere among thousands of genetically modified bacteria, how do we find it?

Gene screening

The first step in finding a gene is to spread the bacteria on a suitable growing medium, such as an agar gel. The individual bacteria then divide, and each one forms a colony containing millions of bacteria. The individuals in each colony are **clones** of the original bacterium. It is easier to test a colony of clones for a particular gene than it is to test a single, tiny bacterium.

It is tricky to look for the gene we want directly, but it is often possible to look for the **protein** it produces. If the bacteria in a colony produce a particular protein, they must have the gene or genes that code for that protein.

If the protein is an **enzyme,** it is reasonably easy to find. Every enzyme controls a particular chemical reaction in a cell. If we provide each bacterial colony with a sample of the enzyme's **substrate,** we can then test each colony for the products of the reaction.

If the protein product is not an enzyme, there are still ways to detect it. Antibodies are proteins produced by the **immune systems** of vertebrates. They are designed to detect foreign protein invaders, bind to them, and then help neutralize them. Each antibody is specific to a particular invader, so it is possible to produce antibodies specific to a particular protein. The antibody becomes the protein detector. Genetic engineers can use antibodies to screen bacterial colonies for proteins they want to find.

Gene probes

Another way to find genes involves the use of **gene probes.** Each gene is unique, with its own sequence of **base** pairs that are not found in any other gene. It is this feature that genetic engineers use to identify genes. First, they make a short stretch of DNA that matches a unique part of the gene they are trying to find. This is the gene probe. The probe is labeled with a **radioactive** material. The DNA in the probe will bind only to the gene the genetic engineers want.

A small sample of each colony is transferred to a nylon filter. These sample colonies are then treated with a strong chemical that causes the bacterial cells to release their DNA. The chemical also causes the two strands of each DNA molecule to separate from one another. The filter is treated to remove any traces of protein, and the single-stranded DNA is baked in place. The filter now has DNA prints, sometimes called DNA ghosts, of all the colonies being tested.

To find out which DNA print the probe has bound to, the filter is brought into contact with a sheet of X-ray film. The radioactivity from the label on the probe causes a dark spot to appear on the film, indicating where the colony in question is located.

This is an X-ray plate used in gene probe detection. The dark spots are fragments of human **chromosome** 17. A defective version of this gene is associated with breast cancer.

Turning to Phages Again

Bacteriophages, or **phages,** are **viruses** that attack bacteria. We learned about them when we looked at **restriction enzymes,** bacteria's defense against a viral attack. Restriction enzymes have proved to be a powerful tool for the genetic engineer, but so too are the phages themselves, as well as other types of viruses.

Phage delivery systems

Bacteriophages and other types of viruses work by inserting their **DNA** into a host cell and hijacking the cell machinery to make copies of the virus. The host cell makes copies of the viral DNA and transcribes the viral genes to make the **proteins** that form the virus's outer coat. The viral proteins and DNA are then assembled into new viruses. This is the only way a virus can reproduce. Outside a host cell, a virus is basically lifeless.

Genetic engineers can use phages as carriers, instead of **plasmids,** to insert foreign DNA into bacterial cells. As with plasmids, restriction enzymes can be used to cut open the DNA and splice in new **genes.** The **recombinant viruses** that form are then used to infect a colony of bacteria. Each phage infects a bacterium and reproduces inside it. The new phages contain copies of the inserted gene. Eventually the bacterial cell is so full of viral copies that it splits open. The released phages go on to infect other bacteria in the colony, until there are billions of copies of the recombinant viruses. The viruses containing the genes that genetic engineers are interested in can then be isolated.

One advantage of inserting genes using phages rather than plasmids is that phages can be made to carry longer lengths of foreign DNA than plasmids can. Phages are often used to construct gene libraries because the DNA needs to be split into fewer fragments. This means that fewer colonies of **clones** need to be made. This makes it easier to find the bacterial colony that contains the protein genetic engineers want to find.

This is the DNA of a bacteriophage. Magnification approx. x 50,000.

Other hosts

Although *E. coli* was the first host cell used by genetic researchers, it is by no means the only one. No cell is immune from an attack by viruses, so viruses can be used to carry foreign DNA into any type of **prokaryote** or **eukaryote** cell.

Viruses can be modified to transfer genes into the host cell's own DNA, instead of making new viruses. When the host cell divides, it not only replicates its own DNA but also the recombinant viral DNA that has been added to it.

Sometimes a virus can take on a plasmidlike existence inside the host cell. The virus can replicate the host cell's DNA plus the spliced-in foreign genes independently of the host cell's **chromosomes.** These "plasmids" are then passed on to the next generation when the host cell divides. However, no virus particles are produced, and the host cell is left unharmed.

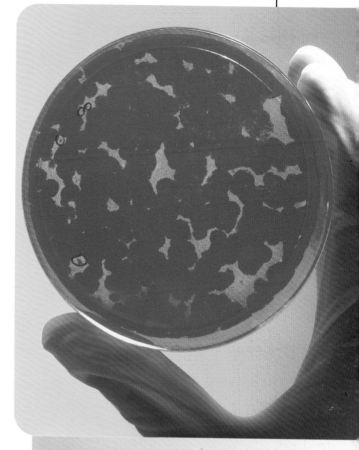

This tissue culture of skin provides a way of testing new drugs without using living **organisms.**

Stepping up

So far we have only discussed genetically altering single cells. This is mainly done to set up microbe factories that can produce a protein that genetic engineers want to have in large quantities, such as insulin. Or, it might be done to improve a cell. It could make a bacterium a more efficient consumer of petrochemical wastes, for example, or alter yeast cells to make them more efficient producers of alcoholic beverages.

Animal and plant cells can be grown in tissue cultures by taking cells from plant and animal tissues and growing them in the laboratory. These tissue cultures can also be genetically engineered. Animal tissue cultures are used in the production of **vaccines** for some viruses, for example. However, this is quite different from producing genetically engineered multicellular organisms. Next we will look at the techniques involved in producing genetically modified plants and animals.

5 Going Multicellular

In some ways, the methods used to genetically engineer multicellular plants and animals are similar to those used for single-celled **organisms.** Of course, there are differences between the two. A multicellular organism is made up of many millions of cells. To change the **genome** of a multicellular organism, we need to be able to introduce the new genes into every one of its cells in such a way that the new genes are passed on whenever cell division takes place.

These plantlets of the tobacco plant (*Nicotinia tabacum*) were grown from callus cells. Each callus cell has the potential to form a complete new plant.

We also want the change to be passed on from generation to generation when the organism reproduces. Most living things reproduce sexually, not by simply dividing as bacteria do. This means that offspring inherit their **genes** from two parents. Each parent forms special sex cells, called **gametes,** with half the number of genes, that combine to form a new organism. Any altered **DNA** needs to be present in these gametes if it is to be passed on to offspring.

Although each cell in a multicellular organism carries the same genes, not all genes are expressed at all times or in all cells. It is therefore important that any introduced genes be appropriately placed. We would not want the foreign gene to be expressed unnecessarily, or perhaps not at all. For example, if researchers introduced a gene into a plant that improved water uptake by the roots, they would not want the plant to waste energy by having its leaves pointlessly produce the **protein** as well.

Plant regeneration

Plants have a remarkable ability to regenerate themselves. A single cell or small pieces of plant tissue can be persuaded to grow into a whole plant. One way of doing this is from a clump of cells called a **callus.** A callus is a group of **undifferentiated** plant cells. These cells are all the same and have no specialized functions. The cells in a callus are attached to each other. They are not a colony of single cells, but they can be separated from each other. Given the right conditions, each cell will form a new

These vanilla plants (*Vanilla plantifolia*) are **clones.** They have been grown from the cells of a single parent plant.

callus. Each new callus can then be treated with plant hormones and encouraged to grow into a new plantlet. When these plantlets are planted and allowed to grow, they develop into mature plants. In this way, we can produce many clones of a single plant.

Producing plant clones in this way has many advantages over growing plants from seed. Plants with superior characteristics, such as larger fruits, can be cloned in this way. All the clones share the original plant's characteristics. Although this is one way of taking control of the reproduction of the plant to gain a particular result, it is actually highly selective breeding rather than real genetic engineering.

The advantage of generating plant clones from the genetic engineer's point of view is simple. If we can insert foreign genes into a group of callus cells, then it is reasonably straightforward to produce genetically altered mature plants from these cells. There remains the problem of getting the foreign genes into the callus cells. In fact, nature is one step ahead of us. Genetic engineers have been able to take advantage of a process that already exists for getting genes into callus cells.

Nature's Genetic Engineer

Many plants, including potatoes, beans, and most trees, can be affected by a condition called crown **gall** disease. It causes a lump, or gall, to appear at the site of a wound. The cause of the disease is a soil bacterium called *Agrobacterium tumefaciens.*

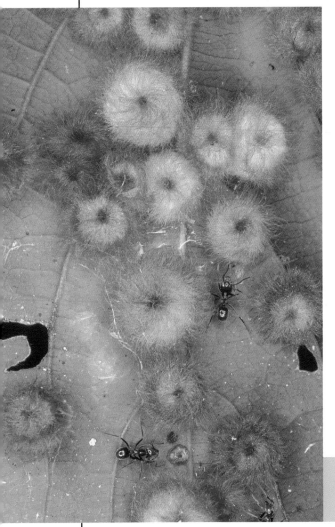

Crown galls appear on the underside of these damaged tree leaves.

A gall is a mass of **undifferentiated** plant cells, like a **callus.** It is also similar to a cancer tumor in a person—a mass of cells that grows out of control. Even when the callus is removed from the plant and cultivated in the laboratory away from the bacterium, it remains tumorous. The tumor cells make substances called **opines,** which are not found in healthy plant cells.

Agrobacterium tumefaciens uses opines as its main nutrient and source of energy. Only this bacterium can use opines in this way. Other soil microbes lack the **enzymes** needed to break down opines. Therefore, only this particular species of bacterium gains an advantage from the plant tumor. When the bacterium infects a plant, it genetically engineers the plant cells to produce tumorous cells, which provide it with a source of food.

The return of the plasmids

Agrobacterium tumefaciens uses **plasmids** to cause, or induce, tumors in the plant. These are called **Ti (tumor-inducing) plasmids.** The bacterium causes healthy plant cells to change into opine-producing tumor cells by transferring Ti plasmids into them. Once the Ti plasmid has been introduced into the plant cell, part of it gets mixed into the plant cell's **DNA.** The plasmid DNA transferred to the plant contains genes that code for **proteins** involved in gall formation and another **gene** that is needed for making opines. The bacterium has effectively achieved with the plant cells what genetic engineers have been doing with bacteria. It has converted them into factories to produce a product it can use.

It is not difficult for the genetic engineer to latch on to *Agrobacterium*'s success in transferring DNA from one species to another. It is a fairly straightforward process to snip out the genes in the plasmid that cause tumor formation and replace them with genes that do things we want them to. The genetically altered bacterium is then used to infect plant tissue, and the foreign genes are taken into the plant's DNA as before. It is not necessary to infect every cell in a plant, because whole plants can be regenerated from infected cells in the same way as they are grown from callus cells.

In nature, *Agrobacterium tumefaciens* only infects dicotyledons, or **dicots.** These are plants that have two leaves, called **cotyledons,** in their seeds. They include beans, peas, and potatoes. Many vital food crops, such as rice and wheat, are **monocots.** Genetic engineers are working to find a way to alter the bacterium so that it infects monocotyledons as well as dicotyledons.

Expressing the new genes

It is not enough just to transfer genes into a plant. Plant genes are often controlled by sequences of DNA that lie next to the gene. These sequences need to be transferred with the gene if it is to be expressed in the plant cell. It is possible, by attaching the right sequences, to have any gene expressed in any plant tissue.

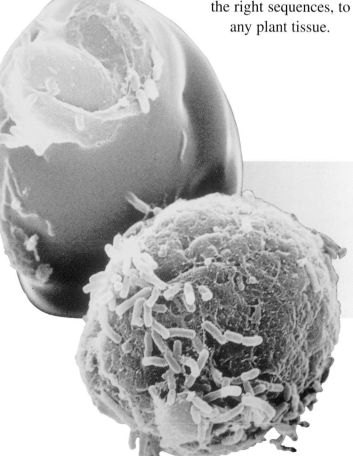

Agrobacterium tumefaciens bacteria grows on the surface of tobacco plant cells. Magnification approx. x 26,000.

Designer Plants

Using *Agrobacterium tumefaciens* is not the only way to get new **genes** into plant cells. Another method involves getting plant cells to take up foreign **DNA** directly, in the same way that bacterial cells can take up **plasmids.** The difficulty is that the plant cell's tough outer wall first has to be removed. This can be done with **enzymes** that break down the cellulose and other materials in the cell wall.

A plant cell with its cell wall removed is called a **protoplast.** Foreign DNA can be introduced into a protoplast in a variety of ways, including with electric shock or with chemicals. After new genes have been introduced, protoplasts regrow their cell walls, which takes about a week. The plant cells can then be regenerated to produce genetically engineered plants.

Better plants

Regeneration has not been as successful with **monocot** cereal plants, such as wheat and corn, as it has been with **dicots,** like carrots and potatoes. However, it can be done, and genetically engineered rice, corn, and other crops are now a reality. For example, genetic engineers have produced improved varieties that offer greater yields.

Other plants have been genetically engineered to produce less lignin. Lignin is a tough chemical that strengthens plant cell walls in woody tissues. It has to be chemically removed from wood that is used to make paper, so trees engineered to contain less lignin would be very useful to the paper industry.

Plants genetically engineered to be resistant to powerful herbicides, or weed killers, are perhaps the most common type of genetically modified crop. By growing these crops, farmers can use high levels of herbicides to kill weeds that grow around the crops without harming the crops themselves.

Some people have doubts about the use of genetically modified plants in food. In many countries, research is under way to ensure that such crops are safe.

Aspens are one tree species that has been genetically engineered to produce less lignin. This is a grove of golden aspen trees.

Vitamins and vaccines

Genetic engineers are working to develop plants that can be used to produce medically useful substances such as vitamins, **vaccines,** and human **proteins** such as hemoglobin.

One possibility being explored is growing plants that have been genetically altered to provide essential vitamins for people in developing countries. Approximately 400 million people worldwide suffer from vitamin A deficiency, which can lead to infections and blindness. Genetic engineers have succeeded in modifying seven genes from plants, bacteria, and fungi and introducing them into rice. The result has been new strains of rice that produce the chemical involved in vitamin A formation and contain large amounts of iron. As little as 300 grams of the cooked improved rice should provide almost all the vitamin A a person needs each day.

Another area of research is the development of edible plant vaccines. This could become a simple, cost-effective way to combat disease worldwide. If people could simply eat foods that are part of their normal diet—but are genetically enhanced to carry vaccines—this would avoid all the problems and expense of providing equipment for making, storing, and delivering vaccines in poorer countries, where they are most needed. Bananas are one possible carrier for these vaccines. Genetically engineered potato plants that **immunize** a person against bacteria that cause diarrhea have already been successfully grown and tested.

The tomatoes at the top are normal and have begun to mold. The tomatoes below are the same age but have been genetically modified to be mold-resistant.

Transgenic Animals

Plants or animals that have been genetically altered with foreign genes are said to be **transgenic organisms.** We have seen the methods developed to create transgenic plants. Animals, however, do not have a plant's ability to regenerate from a single cell. So how can transgenic animals be created?

Going to work on the egg

Although adult animals are made up of millions of different cells, every animal starts life as a single cell—the fertilized egg, or zygote. As the animal grows, whether inside an eggshell or inside its mother, this single cell divides again and again. As more and more cells form, they differentiate to produce all the various cells and tissues and organs that make up the mature animal. When genetic engineers place a new **gene** or genes into an animal, they want to be sure that every cell in the animal contains the new piece of **DNA.** The simplest way to do this is to add the new DNA to a fertilized egg before it begins to divide. Getting new genes into a fertilized egg involves altering an animal's **gametes** (egg cells in a female, sperm cells in a male). These are the only animal cells capable of giving rise to new offspring. All other cells in an animal are called **somatic cells.** Somatic cells are not capable of regenerating into new animals.

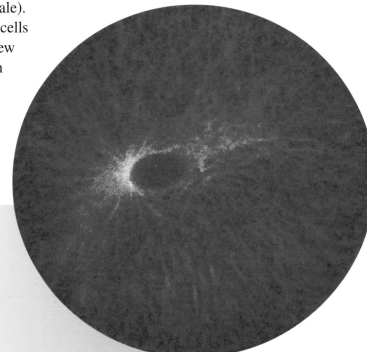

This is the fertilized egg cell of a sea urchin. Any changes made to the DNA will be present in every cell of the adult. Magnification approx. x 1,400.

If the altered DNA is successfully incorporated into a **chromosome** in the **nucleus** of a fertilized egg, it will be copied with the rest of the cell's DNA every time the cell divides. The new DNA will thus be present in every cell of the mature animal. The new DNA may also be present in the mature animal's gametes and so will be passed on to its offspring.

Microinjection

One way to produce a transgenic animal is to use a technique called **microinjection.** Injecting DNA into a fertilized egg is a tricky procedure. Using an ultrafine needle, the new DNA is injected directly into a fertilized egg cell before it starts dividing.

Microinjection is far from 100 percent effective. In most cases, the injected DNA will not be incorporated into a chromosome in the zygote, and none of the cells in the resulting organism will have the new DNA. Other problems can arise with microinjection. Sometimes the new DNA does not get incorporated into a chromosome until after the egg has started to divide. The result is a mosaic animal, which contains the new gene in some of its cells but not in others. Another possibility is that the foreign DNA can disrupt the operation of an important gene in the host cell so that the animal is weakened or dies.

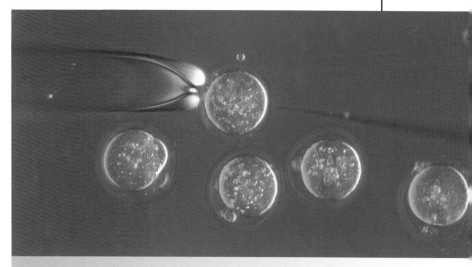

During microinjection, a tiny suction tube (left) holds the cell in place while a very fine needle (right) is used to inject DNA into the cell. Magnification approx. x 1,000.

Microinjection of DNA cannot be carried out within the animal. It has to be done in the laboratory. Once the DNA has been injected, each egg has to be implanted into the **uterus** of another female of the same species who will act as a **surrogate mother.** Only a small number of the implanted eggs will develop successfully into mature, healthy individuals.

The time and effort involved in creating transgenic animals makes it nearly impossible to produce thousands of mature animals and then test each one to see if it is carrying certain genes. Instead, the desired gene has to be **cloned** in advance, using bacteria or cell cultures to find it. Once researchers have a supply of cloned cells containing the gene, the cells can be used as a source of the gene for microinjection.

Transgenic Applications

Researchers have developed **transgenic** animals that have inherited diseases similar to some of those that affect humans. Researchers use these animals to study the progress and symptoms of a disease. They can also be used to test potential new drugs and treatments more safely and inexpensively than can be done with human volunteers. The majority of the transgenic animals developed for this purpose are mice, because they are small and easy to manage and maintain. However, other animals such as rats, rabbits, and pigs have also been used for disease studies.

Ethics and OncoMouse

In 1988 the DuPont pharmaceutical company was granted a patent on a transgenic mouse called OncoMouse. It was given certain faulty genes, called oncogenes, which ensured that it would develop cancers. OncoMice are now used all over the world to test drugs and therapies against cancer.

Other transgenic animals have since been developed for such diseases as **AIDS,** heart disease, and **diabetes.** While the diseases that have been introduced into the mice closely resemble those in humans, there are differences, and this limits the benefits of the mice for research into human cancers. Because of these differences, scientists need to be careful about drawing conclusions about the treatment of a human disease based on the study of transgenic animals.

While naturally the scientists involved would say these studies were carried out with the best of intentions—to rid humans of a terrible disease—there are others who would say that it is wrong to inflict suffering on animals for the benefit of humans. Genetic engineering also raises ethical questions on broader issues such as whether or not we have any right to interfere with nature by designing new **organisms.** The idea of patenting an animal and claiming rights of ownership over it also upsets many people.

This newborn genetically modified mouse contains jellyfish genes that manufacture a protein called GFP (green fluorescent protein). The GFP is what makes the mouse glow green. It is hoped that GFP can be used to mark cancer cells so that scientists can study them.

Research in genetics

Transgenic organisms have been developed to allow scientists to study the structure of **genes** and how they work. They are used to study what effects specific genetic changes have on the characteristics of the whole animal. Transgenic zebra fish are used to study how genes are activated during the development of the **embryo.** Human and fish development actually have many similarities, and so understanding the embryonic development of this fish can also help with the understanding of human development. Developmental genes in humans have similar functions to those in the zebra fish.

Drugs, pigs, and spider goats

The drugs that are used to treat some diseases are simply human **proteins.** It is very expensive to obtain these proteins from other humans, and many of them cannot be produced properly by bacteria. For this reason, researchers are beginning to use transgenic animals that can produce complex human proteins in their milk at relatively low cost. Transgenic goats have been developed to produce a protein that prevents blood clotting, for example. Other transgenic goats have been given spider genes and now produce biofilaments, materials that are as strong as steel, in their milk.

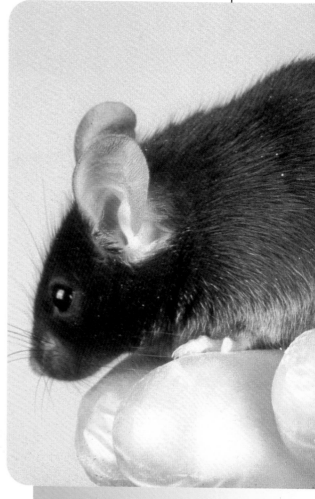

There are many other examples of transgenic animals that could be of benefit to humans. Transgenic pigs grow faster and apparently produce a better quality of meat. These pigs are also more resistant to disease. Transgenic sheep have been developed that grow better wool. However, with all these transgenic animals there are safety concerns. Take the example of transgenic salmon, which have been developed with a gene that increases their growth rate. Farming transgenic salmon commercially would produce bigger fish more quickly. However, there are concerns about the possible effects if transgenic salmon were to escape and breed with wild salmon.

Researchers use this transgenic mouse to study the disease muscular dystrophy. They hope to find the genetic causes of this muscle-wasting disease and develop a therapy to prevent it.

6 Gene Therapy

Genetic engineering research has now made it possible to alter a person's **genes.** Defects in single genes are the cause of more than 3,000 human diseases. **Gene therapy** is a way of treating, curing, or ultimately preventing diseases that result from faulty genes, either by changing the faulty genes or preventing them from being expressed. At present, gene therapy is still in the experimental stage.

If a gene is faulty, the **protein** it codes for will either be faulty or not produced at all. One way to deal with a genetic illness is to provide the patient with a supply of the protein that is lacking. The protein can be made by bacteria that are genetically engineered to carry a copy of the properly functioning human gene. Giving protein in this way is called **replacement therapy,** and it is already widely used. One example of replacement therapy is in people who are born with a faulty gene for a protein called growth hormone. As its name suggests, growth hormone promotes growth. Children with this faulty gene do not grow properly. Without replacement therapy, they would be very short as adults. Replacement therapy works well in this instance because growth hormone affects many sites throughout the body. However, the growth hormone has to be given by injection over a long period. In other genetic diseases, replacement therapy is of limited value because it is difficult to target the specific cells affected by the illness.

These **viruses** have been genetically modified to contain the CFTR gene. A faulty CFTR gene is responsible for the disease **cystic fibrosis.** Researchers want to use the viruses to give cystic fibrosis patients the correct CFTR gene. Magnification approx. x 250,000.

Somatic and germ-line therapies

Gene therapy is a much more direct approach to dealing with genetic illnesses than replacement therapy. Rather than replacing the protein product, gene therapy attempts to replace the faulty gene. It can be targeted either on **somatic cells** or on germ cells (the **gametes**). In somatic gene therapy, the patient's **DNA** is altered but not in such a way that the change is passed on to the next generation. In germ-line gene therapy, egg and sperm cells are changed, with the goal of passing on the changes to the offspring. Germ-line gene therapy is controversial because it means allowing new genes to enter the human gene pool.

Many problems stand in the way of the development of successful gene therapy techniques. One problem is finding a reliable way to get the replacement gene into the body's cells. Currently, **viruses** are the most common means of doing this. Viruses can be engineered to deliver packages of genes into cells. Viruses are an effective way of adding genes into cells, but there can be problems. The body's **immune system** may still recognize the viruses as invaders. And this triggers inflammation and other disease responses.

Researchers are also experimenting with other approaches. One is to introduce an artificial **chromosome** into the body's cells. It would take its place alongside the normal chromosomes and would not interfere with them or cause any **mutations.** It would be capable of carrying substantial amounts of **genetic code,** and would not be attacked by the immune system.

Trials in humans

Another problem with gene therapy is knowing what specific genes do. There are about 30,000 genes in the human **genome,** and scientists know the function of only a few. Genes may have more than one function if they work together with other genes, and some genetic illnesses are caused by more than one gene. In addition it is difficult to target specific cells, and the inserted gene may interfere with the expression of a normal gene. Attempting gene therapy without knowing how everything works could lead to complications.

Most diseases involve the interaction of several genes and the environment. Many people who develop cancer have inherited the gene for the disorder, but environmental factors, such as diet or smoking, may also contribute to the onset of the disease.

This child, at Necker Children's Hospital in Paris, was one of the first patients to receive gene therapy. His immune system did not work properly due to a faulty gene. Scientists introduced genetically engineered white blood cells into his body to correct this potentially fatal condition.

Stem Cells

Stem cells are **undifferentiated** cells that can divide indefinitely and can give rise to more specialized tissue cells. A fertilized human egg cell is a type of stem cell that is described as being totipotent, meaning its potential is total. It has the potential to form an entire **organism.** In the first hours after fertilization, this cell divides into two identical totipotent cells. About four days after fertilization and after several more cell divisions, these totipotent cells begin to specialize. They form a hollow sphere of cells called a **blastocyst.**

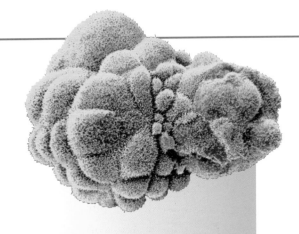

A human embryo at the blastocyst stage, six days after fertilization. Some of the blastocyst cells will form the placenta, others will form the embryo itself. Magnification approx. x 1,500.

The outer layer of the blastocyst forms the **placenta,** which nourishes the **embryo** in the **uterus.** The inner layer of the blastocyst forms the many different tissues of the embryo. Although the cells in the inner layer of the blastocyst can form the embryo, they cannot give rise to the placenta. These cells are now said to be pluripotent. They can give rise to many, but not all types of cells.

The pluripotent stem cells become more specialized and give rise to cells that have a particular function. For example, blood stem cells develop into red blood cells, white blood cells, and platelets, disk-shaped cell fragments that are important for blood clotting. These more specialized stem cells are called multipotent.

Multipotent stem cells are found in the body throughout life. Their job is to replace cells lost through natural wear and tear. For example, blood stem cells are found in the bone marrow and in very small numbers in the bloodstream. Their job is to produce new red blood cells, white blood cells, and platelets to replace cells lost through wear and tear.

Using stem cells

There are a great many ways in which stem cells could be used. One exciting possibility is that embryonic stem cells could be used as universal human donor cells which would be able to provide new liver cells, heart cells, or nerve cells to replace tissues that have been lost or damaged. It may also be possible to treat diseases such as **diabetes, Parkinson's disease,** and **Alzheimer's disease.**

Embryonic stem cells could also be used to provide a source of normal human cells of virtually any tissue type for use in drug screening. Embryonic stem cells seem to be immortal when grown in the laboratory. They continue to divide again and again, without aging.

Obtaining stem cells

Stem cell research faces a major problem because currently the only source of pluripotent human cells is a human embryo. During fertility treatment on women who have problems having children, fertility clinics routinely fertilize more than one egg cell. This means that thousands of unwanted embryos are stored in clinic freezers. Such embryos can be used to produce cultures of stem cells. Obtaining cells in this way is highly controversial, however. Many people have problems with what they see as the destruction of potential human life.

Until recently it was thought that multipotent stem cells from adult tissue could produce only a limited number of cell types. Blood stem cells, for instance, could produce only blood cells. However, experiments with mice suggest that neural, or nerve, stem cells may be able to produce a variety of blood cell types if they are placed in the bone marrow. In addition, studies with rats suggest that stem cells found in the bone marrow are able to produce liver cells. If multipotent cells can be persuaded to produce a wider range of cell types, it will be possible to use adult stem cells for cell therapies and perhaps avoid the need to use stem cells from human embryos.

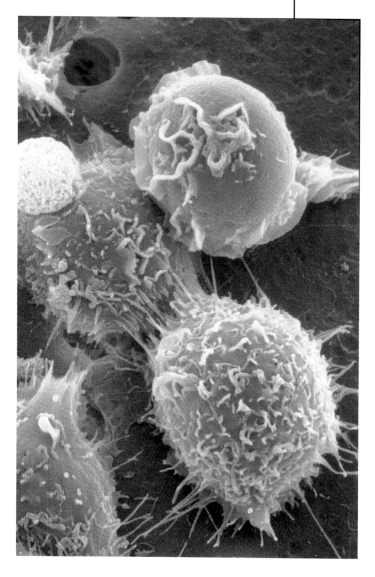

These cells are blood stem cells from human bone marrow. Magnification approx. x 6,800.

Making Clones

Clones are a group of **organisms** that are genetically identical. There are many such organisms in nature that result from **asexual reproduction,** in which a new organism develops from only one parent. Strawberries and other plants that grow from runners are genetically identical to the parent plant, for example. Gardeners often use such techniques as cutting and grafting to produce clones of plants. All the offspring of a single parent are clones. Identical twins are also clones. Both twins develop from the same fertilized egg.

Identical twins are natural clones. Identical twins are formed when a fertilized egg cell splits in two, and both cells grow and develop separately.

The clone arrangers

In July 1996, a team of Scottish scientists produced the first live birth of a healthy sheep cloned from another adult sheep. The team took cells from the udder of one sheep and temporarily starved them for a few days to halt their development. An unfertilized egg was removed from a second sheep, and the **nucleus** was removed. Next, a nucleus from one of the udder cells was transferred into the unfertilized egg. The egg now had a complete set of **genes** from the first sheep. The egg was then grown in the laboratory before being implanted into the womb of a third sheep, the **surrogate mother.** The **embryo** developed normally, and in February 1997, Dolly the sheep was presented to a wondering world.

Transferring a nucleus works because, somehow, some characteristic of the egg cell's **cytoplasm** can reactivate all of the genes in adult cells so that they behave as **stem cells** do. Scientists are trying to figure out how the cloning procedure succeeds in reprogramming adult cells so they act as stem cells. Scientists hope that if they succeed, they might be able to make stem cells of any type from adult tissue.

Practical cloning

Other uses of cloning that have been suggested include the mass production of animals engineered to carry human genes for the production of **proteins** for use as drugs. Mass producing animals with genetically modified organs for use as transplant organs for humans is another possibility. Another is mass producing livestock that have been genetically modified to possess desirable characteristics, such as high milk yield in cows. Cloning could perhaps also be used to save endangered species, although the result would be a genetically weak population because there would be hardly any genetic diversity.

Send in the clones?

Cloning is by no means a certain science. Dolly was the only survivor of 29 embryos implanted into surrogate mothers. Some embryos did not survive, while others were born with serious genetic defects. The structure of Dolly's **chromosomes** also suggests that her life span might be reduced. Other animals such as cattle and mice have been successfully cloned since Dolly, but researchers have had the same problems with large numbers of cloned embryos dying or being born with genetic problems.

Although there are still many unanswered questions about cloning, there are people who think that human cloning is possible. Many childless parents would be willing to try cloning as a way of having a child. However, the majority of genetics scientists feel strongly that we need to understand a lot more about cloning before it will be safe to use in humans.

These five genetically engineered sheep clones were not made by **microinjection,** like Dolly. Instead, a normally fertilized egg was removed from the sheep after only a few divisions. The cells that had formed from the initial egg cell were then separated and placed in surrogate mothers.

7 A Genetic Map

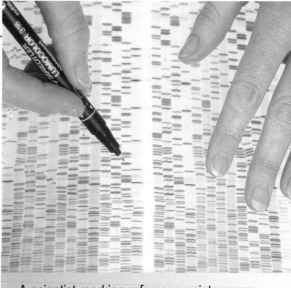

In 1990, a massive international research program called the Human Genome Project set out to identify all of the approximately 30,000 **genes** in human **DNA** (the human **genome**) and to determine the sequence of the three billion or so **base** pairs that make up human DNA. A working draft covering 90 percent of the genome was completed in 2000, by the government-sponsored Human Genome Project and by a private company. By 2003, they will finish the sequence with an accuracy of greater than 99.99 percent.

A scientist marking reference points on an X-ray showing DNA sequences. The reference points allow scientists to work out how different sections of the sequence fit together, like pieces of a jigsaw.

In addition to mapping human DNA, researchers are reading the genomes of several other **organisms** including *Escherichia coli*, the fruit fly, and the mouse. Even species as seemingly different from us as yeast and fruit flies share many similar genes. Valuable information about human diseases can be gained by studying the role of a similar gene in the fruit fly. For example, the role of some human genes in cancer is now understood because scientists have studied related genes in flies. In these studies they found that many of these cancer genes are involved in guiding the development of the **embryo.**

The information gained by mapping the genome has been extemely valuable to geneticists working on genetic illnesses. For example, by 1989 geneticists had tracked down only four genes associated with disease by slowly sorting through the genetic relationships among sufferers. By 1998, more than 100 genes had been pinpointed. The gene for **cystic fibrosis** was found in 1989, after a nine-year hunt. In 1997, the gene for **Parkinson's disease** was identified in just nine days and precisely described within nine months.

Researchers can electronically scan long stretches of DNA to find genes in the sequence that may be responsible for a particular disease. These are called **candidate genes.** If a candidate gene actually does play a role in a disease, the sequence of its base pairs should be different in people with the disease. This difference can be minor. Parkinson's disease can result from a change in just a single **base** pair, which means that just one of the 140 **amino acids** that make up a key **protein** is altered and prevents the protein from doing its job.

Cystic fibrosis

Knowing the DNA sequence of a gene, and, therefore, the sequence of the amino acids it codes for, sometimes allows researchers to figure out the shape and possibly the function of the protein it produces. For instance, when scientists discovered the gene for cystic fibrosis, they recognized it as coding for one of the proteins embedded in the membrane of a cell. These proteins act as gateways and allow certain substances to pass in and out of the cell. It also seemed likely that the protein's task was to allow chloride ions to pass out of the membrane. In cystic fibrosis this protein no longer works properly, and this has far-ranging results. Digestive **enzymes** clog a duct between the pancreas and the small intestine, and food can no longer be digested properly. Thick mucus builds up in the respiratory tract, which can cause repeated lung infections. Cysts that are saclike swellings form in the pancreas, and it becomes fibrous in appearance, giving the disease its name. Cystic fibrosis is the most common genetic illness affecting Caucasians and is always fatal.

Although no cure has yet been found for cystic fibrosis, finding the cystic fibrosis gene has been a great advance. Scientists are now investigating the use of **gene therapy** to introduce healthy copies of the gene into the cells of patients with the illness.

Knowing the complete sequence of the human genome will be a remarkable achievement, but it is only a first step. The next step in genome research will be understanding the function of each gene and how the proteins they code for work.

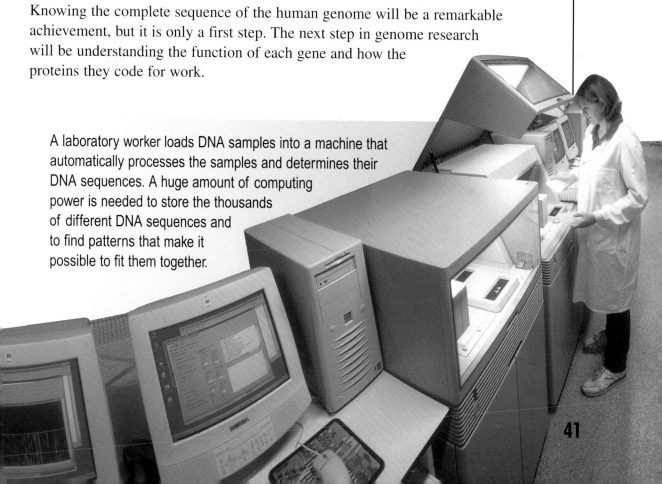

A laboratory worker loads DNA samples into a machine that automatically processes the samples and determines their DNA sequences. A huge amount of computing power is needed to store the thousands of different DNA sequences and to find patterns that make it possible to fit them together.

Genome Challenges

The first phase of the ambitious international Human Genome Project is nearly complete. About three dozen other **organisms,** mostly single-celled microbes, have already had their **DNA** completely sequenced. How much can we expect our knowledge of **genes** to change our lives, if at all? One certain result will be a much greater understanding of biology. Genetic knowledge is already proving useful in developing more effective treatments for many diseases. For instance, the fruit fly, one of the latest organisms to be sequenced, is being used to investigate human disorders such as **Parkinson's disease.**

In the future, a doctor or hospital treating a patient will have the enormous advantage of detailed information about their genetic makeup.

Pharmacogenomics

Pharmacogenomics is the science of using genetic information to predict the safety and effectiveness of a drug taken by a particular individual. A person's medical records may in the future include the complete **base** sequence of their **genome** and a catalog of their genes. It will be possible to use this genetic information to predict how that person will respond to certain drugs and to other substances such as pollutants in the environment. This means that it will be possible to treat each person as a unique genetic individual. Medical treatments will be more specifically tailored to the individual and so will have a greater chance of success. In addition, each person will know his or her genetic weaknesses. This will give him or her the chance to make lifestyle changes to avoid developing illnesses such as heart disease or allergies to certain foods.

Many people die each year from bad reactions to drugs, and millions more suffer uncomfortable side effects. As scientists begin to identify genes that influence drug response, the number of bad reactions should be greatly reduced. Drug treatments sometimes fail because patients lack the gene that allows the body to use the drug effectively. Knowing in advance whether or not this will happen would give doctors and patients the ability to avoid wasting time and money on ineffective treatments and go straight to the drug with the best chance of working.

Life, but not as we know it?

There are some possible problems with knowing about individual genetic differences. It is not too hard to imagine a society in which the DNA of every child born is mapped and stored on a vast computer database. It is already possible to use a process called DNA fingerprinting to tell, with almost complete certainty, whether two samples of DNA are from the same person. Police use this technique to check whether small amounts of DNA, for instance from a person's skin, found at a crime scene match the DNA of a suspect. If everyone's DNA sequence was already held on a computer database, it would be easier to match the DNA from a crime scene to a name on the database. However, many people feel strongly that holding such information about them would be a restriction of their personal freedom.

These people are comparing DNA fingerprints. These fingerprints are from two parents and their child. Technicians identify sequences common to the mother and child (red) and the father and child (blue). DNA fingerprints can prove conclusively whether or not people are related.

Another problem is the possibility that a person's genetic information would be made available to insurance companies or employers. Insurance companies might charge more to insure people who are more likely to get particular diseases. They could do this even though the person is not presently ill. Employers might even avoid hiring people who could possibly fall seriously ill in the future.

Genetic engineers already have the knowledge to create synthetic genes by splicing together DNA **nucleotides.** As our knowledge of genes and development increases, it may become possible for scientists to create from scratch, in the laboratory, a fully functioning living cell. This might seem an exciting prospect, but it also raises serious worries. Do we really know enough about living things and how they work to be comfortable creating what would effectively be a new form of life?

Genetic engineering has many benefits, but it can also cause serious problems. The more we understand about the uses and limits of genetic engineering, the better we will be at making the difficult decisions of what we would like to see it used for and what is not acceptable.

Some Major Events in Genetics

1856	Austrian monk and botanist Gregor Mendel starts his breeding experiments on peas (which will lead him to state the laws of heredity).
1858	English naturalists Charles Darwin and Alfred Russel Wallace announce the theory of Natural Selection, which states that individuals that are better adapted to their environment survive, reproduce and pass on their characteristics
1859	Darwin publishes *The Origin of Species.*
1866	Mendel publishes the results of his investigations on inheritance in pea plants.
1871	Nitrogen and phosphorous material discovered in cell nuclei, now known as the genetic material DNA.
1873	First accurate description of mitosis is offered.
1900	Mendel's principles are independently discovered and verified by several scientists, marking the beginning of modern genetics.
1902	**Chromosomes** are identified as carriers of genes when cell division is shown to be associated with heredity.
1920s	Major component of chromosomes is shown to be DNA.
1944	Role of DNA in genetic inheritance is first demonstrated by biologist Oswald Avery.
1953	American biologist James Watson and English molecular biologist Francis Crick announce the three-dimensional structure of the DNA molecule as a double helix. They also propose a mechanism for replication of DNA.
1954	Cosmologist George Gamow suggests that the **genetic code** consists of the order of triplets of **bases** in the DNA molecule.
1956	Humans shown to have 23 pairs of chromosomes.
1958	Geneticists show that genes act by regulating definite chemical events in the cell.
1966	Genetic code is cracked when it is shown that DNA has triplet **codons** that specify each of the twenty **amino acids.**
1969	Geneticists isolate a single gene for the first time.
1973	Scientists develop technique of **recombinant DNA.** This marks the beginning of genetic engineering.
1981	Insulin made by bacteria is the first genetically engineered product to go on sale.
1984	British geneticist Alec Jeffreys develops genetic fingerprinting technique of identifying individuals (as DNA pattern is unique to each person).
1988	Human Genome Project begins, with the goal of determining the entire sequence of bases in human DNA.
1990	First successful **gene therapy** carried out in the United States for a girl with SCID—a rare immunodeficiency disease caused by a genetic defect.
1993	Flavr Savr tomatoes, the first genetically engineered food (for longer shelf life), are marketed.
1997	Scottish geneticists at the Roslin Institute **clone** a sheep (called Dolly).
1999	Base sequence of human chromosome 22 announced. There are more than 500 genes.
2000	Human Genome Project presents its preliminary results. Each of the body's 10 trillion cells contains some 3.1 billion base units—only one percent of these are thought to be transcribed. We may have as few as 30,000 genes!

Glossary

agar gel jellylike substance made from seaweed used as a growth medium for bacteria

AIDS (acquired immune deficiency syndrome) serious viral disease

Alzheimer's disease disease that causes memory loss, poor mental ability, and eventually physical problems

amino acid naturally occurring chemical used by cells to make **proteins**

antibiotics chemicals that destroy or stop the growth of disease-causing bacteria

asexual reproduction reproduction in which an **organism** produces genetically identical copies of itself

bacteriophage (phage) virus that infects bacteria

base type of chemical found in genetic material. There are four different bases in DNA.

blastocyst hollow, fluid-filled ball of cells that is an early stage in the growth of a fertilized human egg.

callus growth of unspecialized cells that forms over a wound in a plant

candidate gene gene that may be the site of a particular genetic disease

catalyst substance that speeds up a chemical reaction

chromosome DNA molecule coiled around protein molecules

clone organism that is genetically identical to another

codon sequence of three bases that together code for a particular amino acid

cotyledon structure in a plant seed that becomes one of the plant's first leaves or acts as a food store

cystic fibrosis disease caused by a faulty gene that involves large amounts of mucus production, especially in the lungs

cytoplasm all the contents of a cell outside the **nucleus**

deoxyribonucleic acid see DNA

diabetes disease caused by a lack of the hormone insulin, in which there is no control over the levels of sugar in the blood

dicot (dicotyledon) type of plant that has two cotyledons or seed leaves

DNA (deoxyribonucleic acid) genetic material of living things that carries instructions for constructing, maintaining, and reproducing living cells

DNA polymerase enzyme involved in replicating one strand of DNA from another

embryo very young organism in the early stages of development, before it emerges from the egg or seed or is born from its mother

enzyme type of protein that controls one of the thousands of chemical reactions inside a living cell. Enzymes are catalysts.

eukaryote cell that has a membrane-enclosed nucleus. All kinds of living things except bacteria are made up of eukaryote cells.

exon section of DNA that codes for a protein

gall swelling produced on a plant caused by the attack of a parasite

gamete sex cell in organisms that reproduce sexually

gene section of DNA that contains the information to make all or part of a protein

gene expression production of a protein from a gene or genes. When a gene is expressed, it gives rise to characteristics in the organism, such as pink flowers in a pea plant or curly hair in a child.

gene probe short section of DNA whose sequence of bases matches up with a unique part of a particular gene

gene splicing process of cutting open a DNA molecule, inserting a new gene or genes, and then closing it up again

gene therapy treatment for a genetic disease that aims to replace a faulty gene with a properly working one

genetic code way in which the four bases that make up DNA or RNA chains code for the twenty amino acids that make up proteins

genome complete set of genetic information of a particular individual

histone protein in the cell nucleus that is closely associated with DNA

immune system protects an organism from infection and disease

immunize to protect a person against a particular illness by stimulating his or her immune system

intron section of a gene in a eukaryote cell that does not code for a protein or part of a protein

lactose complex sugar made of galactose and glucose

messenger RNA molecule that carries the genetic code for a protein out of the nucleus to where protein assembly takes place

microinjection use of an ultrafine needle to inject DNA into a cell

microorganism single-celled organism that is too small to be seen with the naked eye

monocot type of plant that has one cotyledon or seed leaf

mutation any change in a cell's genes or in a chromosome's structure, or a change in the number of chromosomes in a cell

nucleotide small molecule that joins together in chains to form DNA and RNA molecules

nucleus structure where the cell's genetic material is stored

opine substance made by tumor cells in plants

organism any type of living thing

Parkinson's disease disease of the nervous system in which the muscles become rigid and the patient cannot move

phage see **bacteriophage**

placenta structure produced by the fertilized egg in mammals, that connects to the uterus and obtains nutrients for the growing baby from the mother's blood

plasmid small, circular piece of DNA found in many bacteria

polypeptide large number of amino acids joined together to form one long molecule

prokaryote cell that does not contain a nucleus. Bacteria are prokaryotes.

promoter section of DNA immediately before a gene, where the enzyme responsible for producing messenger RNA for that gene attaches

protein substance that makes up many cell parts and controls a cell's reactions.

protoplast plant cell without its cell wall

radioactive state in which the atoms of a substance gradually break down, emitting some kind of radiation (high-energy waves or subatomic particles)

recombinant DNA DNA from one source containing some material from another source

recombinant virus virus that contains DNA from another source within its own DNA

regulatory protein controls whether or not a gene is expressed

replacement therapy treatment for a genetic disease in which a protein that is missing because of a faulty gene is injected into the patient

respiration process of obtaining oxygen from the environment to be used in the breakdown and release of energy from food

restriction enzyme cuts DNA molecules at particular points, breaking it up into fragments

reverse transcriptase enzyme that makes it possible to make a DNA molecule from an RNA template

ribonucleic acid see **RNA**

ribosome small structure within a cell that is the site of protein synthesis

RNA (ribonucleic acid) substance related to DNA that plays an important part in protein synthesis

somatic cell any cell in a multicellular organism that is not a reproductive cell

stem cell unspecialized cell that can divide to form several or many different cell types

substrate substance on which an enzyme acts

surrogate mother female that incubates and gives birth to an offspring that is not her own

Ti plasmid small, circular piece of DNA found in the bacterium *Agrobacterium tumefaciens* that causes a plant to grow a gall

totipotent stem cell that is capable of dividing and growing to produce a complete organism

transcription production of a single-stranded RNA molecule from a section of DNA

transfer RNA carries amino acids to the ribosomes and in attaching them to protein chains

transgenic containing a gene or genes from another organism

translation process by which information coded on messenger RNA is transformed into a protein

undifferentiated cell that has not become specialized for a particular task

uterus organ in a female mammal where its offspring develop before birt.

vaccine substance often made of dead or inactivated disease-causing microorganisms, that stimulates the immune system and protects an organism against a disease

virus small section of DNA or RNA surrounded by a protective protein coat

Further Reading

Morgan, Sally. *Science at the Edge, Cloning*. Chicago: Heinemann Library, 2002.

Morgan, Sally. *Science at the Edge, Genetic Modification of Food*. Chicago: Heinemann Library, 2002.

Wallace, Holly. *Life processes: Cells and Systems,* Chicago: Heinemann Library, 2002.

Index